by Katherine Talmadge Sallé

Table of Contents

Introduction

Fire is a natural force. It has always existed. Pieces of petrified wood and coal show traces of fires from 350 million years ago.

A **wildfire** is any unwanted or unplanned fire in a forest or grassland setting. Most people think that wildfires are bad. This isn't always true. Wildfires do destroy forest trees and plants. Very hot fires can even destroy soil. Such destruction leads to the loss of shelter and food for forest creatures. It can also lead to loss of life.

But wildfires can be helpful, too. They clean the forest by burning away dead fallen trees. Even when a fire burns healthy trees, it is helpful. It leads to **succession**. This is a natural process of change. Old trees burn and die, and new trees grow in their place. Thinning the forest also lets sunlight stream in, bringing wildflowers and ferns. Such growth and change make the forest healthier.

Wildfire, then, is both friend and enemy. And just as a pine tree, a ladybug, or a deer is a natural member of the forest, so is the force of wildfire.

Stream - light / water

Sometimes weather patterns make it easier for small fires to spread and grow out of control. Each region of our nation has an annual fire season when most wildfires happen. In the West it is June through October. In the Southeast it is March through May. In the Northeast it is late fall. During these months the weather tends to be hot and dry. **Droughts**, or periods without rain, often occur. Hot, dry winds provide further danger. For example, the Chinook and Santa Ana winds bring fire hazards to western forests. They act like hair dryers, blowing through the forests at high speeds drying everything out.

The shape of the land helps fires to grow. Rising smoke and heat cause fires to burn faster uphill than downhill. For the same reason, fires can jump from short trees to tall trees. In Yosemite National Park rangers learned that fires in short fir trees quickly jumped to giant sequoia trees. By removing the fir trees, the rangers saved the giant sequoias.

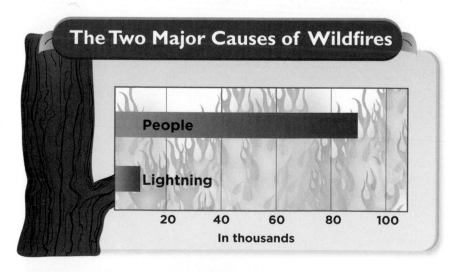

The Two Major Causes of Wildfires

People

Lightning

20   40   60   80   100

In thousands

Keeping Homes Safe

Jackson County, Oregon, was one of the first regions to pass a **firebreak** law. It states that homes in the forest must be surrounded by a 30-foot firebreak. A firebreak is a section of open space that is cut and dug within a forest. Removing all trees and other fuel can stop a fire from advancing.

⌒ Firefighters remove trees and brush around homes in Arizona to stop the spread of a forest fire.

Homeowners also have helped wildfires to spread and grow. More and more people are building homes on forest land. They bring new fuels to the forest, such as gas in their cars and electricity in their homes. Also, they often leave forest trees near their homes. Wildfires can then quickly engulf them. Many regions have passed laws to reduce such dangers.

The most important thing people can do to prevent wildfires is to be more careful. Although lightning starts most natural fires, it starts only 10 percent of all forest fires. People cause the other 90 percent.

Chapter 2

Aftermath of a Wildfire

For many years forest and park rangers thought that all fires were bad. In recent years they have changed their minds. Fire is considered a force that creates change. Some of the change is destructive to the forest. However, some of the change is helpful.

Fire is a powerful, dangerous force. It has destroyed millions of acres of forest and thousands of buildings and homes. Chemicals from burned vehicles and homes pollute streams and lakes. Smoke creates air pollution. And fires cost lots of money—in the loss of personal property and in the funds needed to prevent and fight fires. Fires also cause great losses to forest-based businesses, such as the lumber industry and tourism.

↻ Surface fires like this one move more slowly than crown fires.

↻ This pine seedling has sprouted after a forest fire in Minnesota.

Wildfires also often destroy life. A troop of 49 firefighters were fighting a fire in Colorado in 1994. Suddenly, strong winds caused the flames to shoot toward them, over a distance of 100 feet (30 meters). Thirty-five firefighters survived. Fourteen did not.

Many animals and plants also die during wildfires. But others have ways to survive. Deer, bear, and most other animals run to escape fire. Others, such as mice, snakes, and lizards, burrow deep into the earth. Adult birds fly away, but small chicks and flightless birds often do not escape. Most insects do not escape either.

Plants, of course, cannot flee. But many have features that help them survive. Douglas fir and coast redwood trees have very thick bark. It insulates the tree from the heat of the fire. By contrast, the aspen tree has thin bark. Its trunk usually burns in a wildfire. However, its deep roots survive. After the fire, new saplings emerge from those roots, and the aspen tree grows again.

Prescribed Fires

Your doctor might prescribe medicine if you are sick. In the same way, fire officials might prescribe a fire to a forest that needs help!

Officials set **prescribed fires** for specific goals, such as:

- To burn away dead brush. Then, if a wildfire happens, it will not have as much fuel to burn.

- To burn away old trees to make way for new, healthier ones.

- To make open, sunny spaces where grass can grow, giving deer and other animals more food.

Strict rules govern prescribed fires. They must not be set in dry, windy times. People must watch them at all times. They must make sure the fires stay controlled and do not spread.

Wildfires can also help forests. They clean the forest floor of dead leaves, underbrush, and fallen trees. Ash from a fire enriches the soil with nitrogen and carbon. These nutrients make the surviving plants stronger. They also attract beetles and other insects, providing food for birds. In the sunny spaces that appear in a burned forest, wildflowers and grasses sprout. These provide rich new food for deer and other animals. Even the burned tree trunks are useful. They provide shelter to many animals.

Fires also rid the forest of poison oak and other weeds. And it kills insects that are harmful to trees, including sawflies and maple leaf cutters.

Some forest plants even *need* fires! The jack pine and lodgepole pine are good examples. Their cones are sealed shut with sticky pitch. They need heat in order to open. During a fire the cones open. Then their seeds pour out, settling in the rich, ashy soil. Soon new trees sprout. After the 1988 wildfire at Yellowstone National Park, there were up to one million of these seeds per acre of forest. Some sprouted as new trees, and others provided food for the squirrels, birds, and mice.

↻ After a wildfire, more sunshine reaches the forest floor. That makes it possible for young lodgepole pines to grow.

Chapter 3

Fighting a Wildfire

Fighting fires is dangerous work. It takes a lot of courage and strength. Wildfire crews usually work in shifts. For two weeks they must be available 24 hours a day, 7 days a week. Then they receive two to four days of rest before their next shift. While fighting a fire, they take turns sleeping, often close to the firebreak.

There are usually few roads in the wilderness. Therefore, fire engines cannot get to many wildfires. When fires are spotted, the first firefighters to move in are often **helitacks** or **smokejumpers**.

Helitacks come by helicopter. They land as close to the fire as possible and begin fighting it. Meanwhile, the pilots go on a quest for nearby water sources. Then they come back again and again with bucket drops. These are pails of water hanging from the helicopter on long cables. Planes called air tankers might also drop water.

Planes also bring smokejumpers, who parachute in to fight wildfires. Smokejumpers bring their firefighting tools and supplies in backpacks. Each pack weighs about 100 pounds.

If the wildfire is not out within a few days, new crews of firefighters arrive to help.

Smokejumpers often parachute into very remote areas. They must carry all the food and supplies they need with them.

Hotshots are top-level wildfire crews. They fight the most difficult and dangerous fires.

Twenty people form a hotshot crew. They either fly or hike to remote fires. They carry all their tools and supplies in backpacks. Their training includes hiking three miles with a 45-pound backpack in 45 minutes.

Because they are always in danger, they must have very strong bodies and spirits. The most hazardous fires may create **firestorms**. These are swirling, intensely hot winds, sometimes as strong as a hurricane. They can reach temperatures of 3,600° Fahrenheit (2,000° Celsius).

The Portable Fire Shelter

Along with their tools, forest firefighters carry fire shelters in their packs. This is a lightweight tent folded up into a small pouch. In a life-threatening crisis, the firefighter can set up this tent very quickly and crawl

- How has technology helped people fight fires?

How does technology change life for humans?

The Pulaski

Firefighters have called the pulaski "the greatest fire handtool." It is light enough to be carried in a forest firefighter's backpack, and it is two tools in one. One end of its head is an axe. It is used to cut small trees, branches, and roots. The other end is a hoe. It is used to dig into the ground to cut firebreaks. The pulaski was named after Ed Pulaski, a firefighting hero. He is famous for leading his men to safety during a terrible fire in 1910.

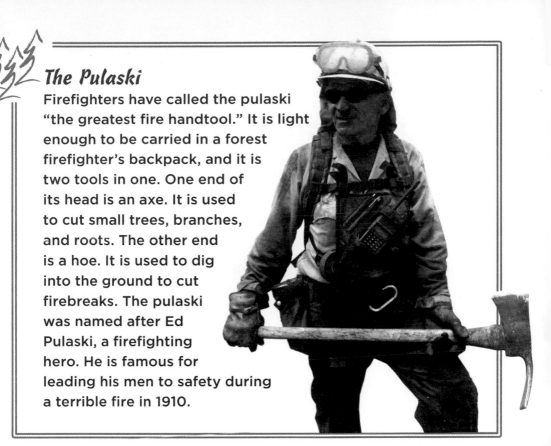

Firefighters wear fire-resistant clothes. These clothes are usually yellow, the color easiest to see. They also wear hardhats and goggles. At night they wear headlamps. In their packs they carry shovels and other tools. They also carry backpack pumps. These are bags fitted with sprayers. Each bag contains about five gallons of water. Firefighters use it to put out small flames.

They also carry radios to talk to each other and to lookouts in planes. However, a roaring fire often makes radios useless. Today, some firefighters use handheld computers that let them "talk" through text messages.

Chapter 4

Two Deadly Fires

Here are the stories of two of our nation's worst wildfires. These two fires happened more than 100 years apart, and the effect of both fires is still felt today. As you read, compare and contrast the two fires. How are they different and how are they alike?

Peshtigo, Wisconsin 1871

In 1871 Peshtigo was a busy frontier town. It was surrounded by thick forests, and lumber was the big business. Many people were moving to town and clearing land for farms and homes. Big wooden houses lined the streets.

The summer of 1871 brought a long drought. The land and air were very hot and dry. To clear land for new homes, people set small fires. The fires smoldered for much of the summer and early fall. Meanwhile, the creeks dried up. The lumber mills dumped sawdust into the dry creek beds. Based on what you have read about fires, you can see what dangers were brewing.

People and animals could not escape the fast-moving flames during the Peshtigo fire. ⊃

On the evening of October 8, strong winds blew in from the west. They buffeted the small fires, and the flames quickly grew. Then the winds swirled into a tornado. When the wind hit the rising flames, it formed a firestorm. It was a twisting wall of flame, about a mile high and five miles wide. It was so strong that it threw train cars into the air. The fire jumped 10 miles across the waters of Green Bay and spread to other towns. It was so hot that it turned sand into glass. Peshtigo was destroyed in just an hour. Only the people who dove into the river survived. One girl held onto the horns of a floating steer all night.

The fire died out by October 9. But it had destroyed 2,400 square miles, an area twice the size of Rhode Island. It destroyed 17 towns and killed more than 1,200 people. When it was over, only one building stood in Peshtigo. This fire happened more than a century ago. But it remains the worst wildfire in our nation's history.

Yellowstone National Park 1988

Yellowstone is our nation's oldest national park. It was founded in 1873. It contains more than 2 million acres of meadows and forest. Most of the park is in Wyoming with small parts in Montana and Idaho.

Each year lightning starts about 24 wildfires in Yellowstone. They are a normal part of its ecosystem. However, the wildfire of 1988 was one of the worst fires in our nation's history. It was really eight fires.

By 1988 most fire experts believed that small fires can help forests. Therefore, they let small wildfires burn. When fires started in Yellowstone, the rangers didn't put them out. But they watched the fires carefully.

Then, like in Peshtigo, dry, gusty winds swirled in. The "helpful" wildfires roared out of control.

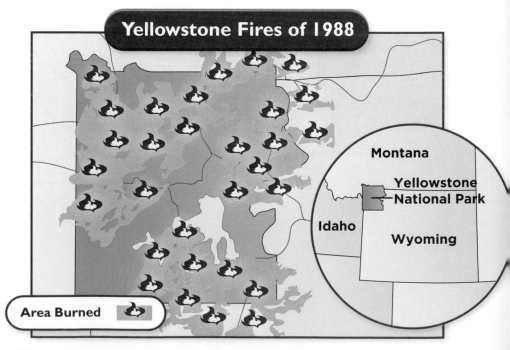

Yellowstone Fires of 1988

Montana

Yellowstone National Park

Idaho

Wyoming

Area Burned

⌒ Smoke from the Yellowstone fires could be seen for hundreds of miles.

A small fire was started by lightning in late June. By July 21 the wildfire had burned 16,600 acres. More than 10,000 men and women pitched in. There were soldiers, helitacks, smokejumpers, and hotshots. But the fire continued to grow. Like the Peshtigo fire, it jumped across water. Firefighters used bulldozers to cut wide firebreaks, but the firebreaks didn't work. High winds blew hot embers as far as 1.5 miles. New fires started where the embers landed. Then firestorms swept up hills. The heat was so strong that trees burned into white ash almost instantly and huge rocks shattered.

The fires raged for weeks. Then on September 10, the weather finally changed. Rain and snow began to fall. Spot fires burned on until November, but the worst was over.

In all, more than one million acres burned. Many buildings in the park and nearby towns were destroyed. Once the fires were out, nature began to rebuild. In a year the burned meadows grew back. In five years the burned forests had new growth.

Conclusion

A wildfire is any unwanted or unplanned fire that burns in a forest or grassland setting. Lightning causes many wildfires. Sadly, people cause them, too.

Forest plants and animals often adapt to fire. Some forest plants have thick bark or deep roots that help them survive. Other forest plants have seeds that need the fire's heat in order to sprout new plants. Most forest animals flee the flames. Then they return to find new shelter and food once the fire is over. Others burrow deep into the soil and wait for the flames to pass by.

🔊 New growth has begun to appear beneath the skeletons of the old forest.

Of course, many plants and animals do not survive wildfires. That seems sad because most people want to protect wildlife. But nature has a larger plan. Fire cleans the forest. It thins out some trees so that others have enough sun and water to live. It thins out the animal population in the same way.

Fire is one of the most powerful forces on Earth. It is both destructive and helpful. But scientists do not judge fire as being good or bad. Instead they think of it as a force that brings changes. An old forest burns and changes into a meadow. Then new growth sprouts. The meadow begins to change back into a forest. Those are steps in a natural cycle. It is a cycle that repeats over and over again. There are no ends. There are only new beginnings.

Glossary

crown fire *(KROUN fighr)* a fire that burns through the tops of trees *(page 5)*

drought *(DROUT)* a long period without rain *(page 6)*

firebreak *(FIGHR-brayk)* (also *fireline*) *(FIGHR-lighn)* a break of open space that is cut and dug ahead of a fire, to remove fuel in the fire's path *(page 7)*

firestorm *(FIGHR-storm)* violent, swirling hot air currents caused by a large, extremely hot fire. A firestorm is a tornado-like column of smoke, debris, and flames. *(page 14)*

ground fire *(GROUND fighr)* a fire that burns plant roots and organic matter in the soil, beneath the surface of the forest floor *(page 5)*

helitack *(HEL-i-tak)* a first-alert wilderness firefighter who is brought in by helicopter *(page 12)*

hotshot *(HOT-shot)* a top-level wilderness firefighter *(page 14)*

prescribed fire *(pri-SKRIGHBD fighr)* a fire that is purposely set to meet a specific goal, such as cleaning out underbrush or improving a habitat *(page 10)*

smokejumper *(SMOHK-jump-ur)* a wilderness firefighter who parachutes into the fire area from an airplane *(page 12)*

succession *(suhk-SESH-uhn)* in wild areas, the slow, regular, and continuous replacement of one type of plant by another, usually due to fire or another natural event *(page 3)*

surface fire *(SUR-fis fighr)* a fire that burns leaf litter, fallen branches, and other fuel located on the forest floor *(page 5)*

wildfire *(WIGHLD-fighr)* any unwanted or unplanned fire burning in forest, shrub, or grassland settings *(page 2)*

Index

Comprehension Check

Summarize

Wildfires are described as being both friend and enemy. Compare the two fires described in the book, the Peshtigo fire and the Yellowstone, and list examples that show how the fires were alike and different. In each case, were the fires friend or enemy?

Think and Compare

1. The author suggests similarities and differences between helitacks, smokejumpers, and hotshots. Reread pages 12–14. Then tell how the members of each group are alike and different. **(Compare and Contrast)**

2. Do you think you would enjoy being a member of a hotshot crew? Explain why or why not. **(Evaluate)**

3. Imagine that a friend said to you, "All fires are terrible." Based on what you have read in this book, what facts might you share with your friend? **(Apply/Evaluate)**